Alateen Talks Back
On
ACCEPTANCE

Al-Anon Family Group Headquarters, Inc.

Alateen, part of the Al-Anon Family Groups, is a fellowship of young people whose lives have been affected by alcoholism in a family member or close friend. We help each other by sharing our experience, strength and hope.

We believe alcoholism is a family disease because it affects all the members emotionally and sometimes physically. Although we cannot change or control our parents, we can detach from their problems while continuing to love them.

We do not discuss religion or become involved with any outside organizations. Our sole topic is the solution of our problems. We are always careful to protect each other's anonymity as well as that of all Al-Anon and AA members.

By applying the Twelve Steps to ourselves, we begin to grow mentally, emotionally and spiritually. We will always be grateful to Alateen for giving us a wonderful, healthy program to live by and enjoy.

Suggested Alateen Preamble to the Twelve Steps

For more information and catalog of literature write:
Al-Anon Family Group Headquarters, Inc.
1600 Corporate Landing Parkway
Virginia Beach, VA 23454-5617
Phone: (757) 563-1600 Fax: (757) 563-1655

All rights reserved. Excerpts from this publication may be reproduced only with the written permission of the publisher.

Al-Anon/Alateen is supported by members' voluntary contributions and from the sale of our Conference Approved Literature.

ISBN-910034-81-8

© AL-ANON FAMILY GROUP HEADQUARTERS, INC. 1992

Approved by
World Service Conference
Al-Anon Family Groups

INTRODUCTION

The articles and artwork in this booklet about ACCEPTANCE, taken from past issues of *Alateen Talk*, have been provided by Alateen members of all ages worldwide. The sharings reinforce the idea that ACCEPTANCE of life as it is, is the first step in dealing with our problems and doing something about them in a healthy, positive way.

ACCEPTANCE comes through the comfort we receive from members at meetings when we slowly begin to understand and care about ourselves and others, and by recognizing that alcoholism is a disease. We come to accept that we can only change ourselves—no one else. Once we have accepted this, we can separate our problems from the disease and begin to show love and compassion for our families and our friends, including the alcoholic.

At the end of this booklet there are ten questions to help us find ACCEPTANCE. We can use them for our personal recovery, or as topics at an Alateen meeting.

Alateen Talk is published quarterly and has been serving the membership since 1961. For information about a subscription to *Alateen Talk*, please write to the address listed in this booklet.

Adam
Vermont, U.S.A.

Today, I am proud of my family. I no longer blame my parents for the disease of alcoholism. They didn't create it, or cause it. They are trying just as hard as I am to deal with it. I simply love them for who they are, and thank God I have them to cherish the rest of my life.

I have so much to be grateful for. Even though alcoholism is in my life, I choose not to live my life depressed and unhappy. I have accepted the disease and that's half the battle. Coping with it, is what's left. I have to live with that challenge the rest of my life; but that's okay because the Twelve Steps give me a path to follow.

Melody
Kentucky, U.S.A.

When I was 13 years old I looked like a wild creature, with my sloppy clothes and my shaggy, uncombed hair that hung in my face.

I had isolated myself from reality, from everyone around me, and I felt so alone. I dreamed of a place to be where I could dress as I wanted and be who I wanted without feeling like I wasn't good enough. I dreamed of a place where people would accept me completely as I was. It would be two years before I found this place. It is called Alateen.

The night I attended my first Alateen meeting, I was lonely and desperate. I felt then, as I had felt my whole life, as if nobody could understand me, nobody had my problems. I thought I was crazy. Most of all, I hated myself. I thought it would be impossible for any of the people in this group to look at me and do anything but turn away. So I would go to one meeting; I would hate them, they would hate me and that would be it. Wrong!

They began to speak, and I completely understood everything I heard—pain, loneliness, rejection and fear. And I knew—I knew that I was home. Those people saw what I put forth, and took me at face value. They did not attach hidden meanings to my words, nor did they judge me for anything I said or did. They simply accepted who I was and listened when I spoke. And they cared. Today those people are my friends. I see them at meetings, dances and parties.

Where once I withdrew and hid, fearing pain and rejection, I am now learning to relax and not be afraid, of who I am. Where once I huddled in a corner and felt as if I would explode for lack of someone to talk to, I now have about 40 phone numbers to call if something goes wrong.

Alateen taught me to take each day as it comes. It showed me that I have no control over others, that all I can change is myself, and that I can't do that all at once. It takes time, it takes a lot of time and a lot of effort, but if I want a life I can enjoy, there is no other alternative. I'm learning to cry, but I'm learning to laugh, too; and I am happier now than I have ever been in my life.

Serra
New York, U.S.A.

Alateen Member
Massachusetts, U.S.A.

Before Alateen, I thought I only had problems coping with my mother. She is the alcoholic in my family. I knew her problem was drinking and mine was a lot of other stuff built up inside of me. I couldn't talk to anybody about it and I couldn't accept her either.

I think her drinking also affected my ability to be responsible. I was supposed to take care of my younger sister but I wasn't able to be responsible enough. I also had a paper route. I didn't do a very good job with this either.

One day, my father, who is in Al-Anon, took me to an open Alateen meeting at a conference. Later, I went to a group meeting. I didn't like Alateen at first, but then I started to listen to everyone. As they were talking, I learned they all had the same problems as me. Now I know my mom drinks because she has a disease. I have been able to accept it. Now, I'm glad to be in Alateen.

Ann
Ontario, Canada

I am 13 years old and I have been coming to Alateen for two years, and I have learned a lot. I have learned how to cope with problems and I can't change anyone but myself. I have also learned and accepted that the alcoholic has a sickness, and it affects the whole family, not just him. Since I started coming to Alateen I have met a lot of friends. When I came to my first meeting, my mother forced me to go, but soon after that, I wanted to come to the meetings. I learn a lot from the people I meet here.

S.M.B.
Ohio, U.S.A.

I had hated my alcoholic parent for a long time, but since I've been in Alateen, a short eleven weeks, I no longer have such contempt...just an understanding and an ever growing love that I've never held before. I have also learned that the only person I can change is myself and I am trying to do this now. Each day has become separate and distinct, making my life much fuller.

Sandy
Missouri, U.S.A.

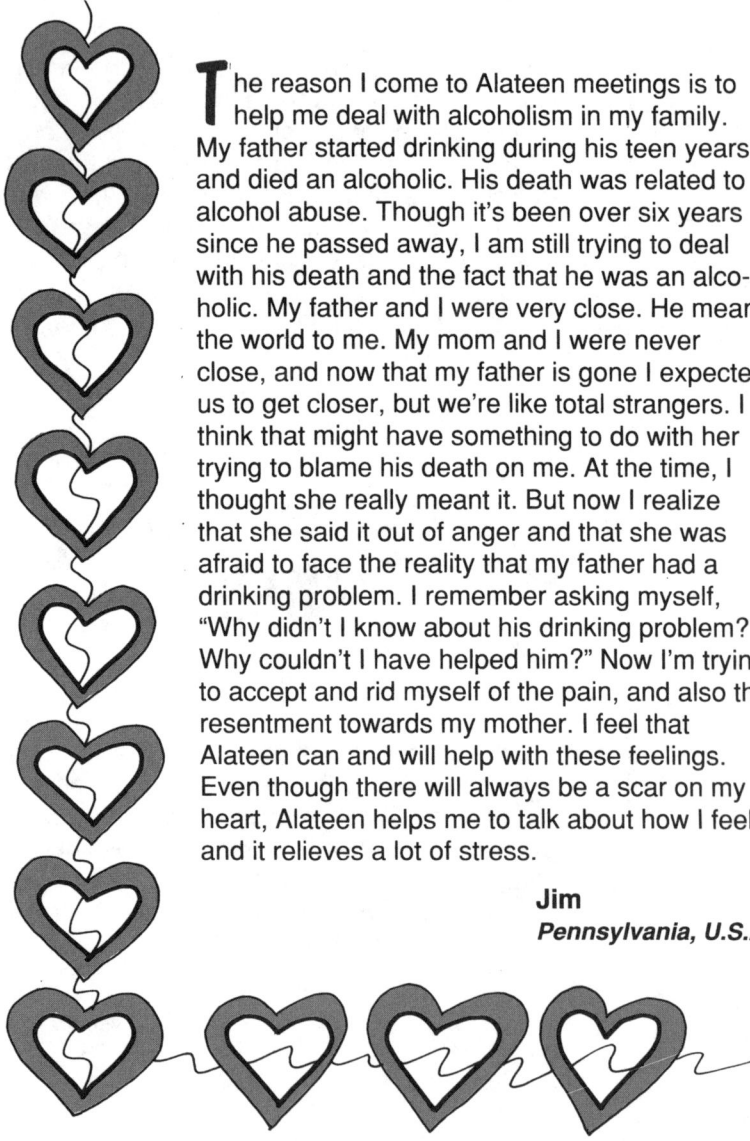

The reason I come to Alateen meetings is to help me deal with alcoholism in my family. My father started drinking during his teen years and died an alcoholic. His death was related to alcohol abuse. Though it's been over six years since he passed away, I am still trying to deal with his death and the fact that he was an alcoholic. My father and I were very close. He meant the world to me. My mom and I were never close, and now that my father is gone I expected us to get closer, but we're like total strangers. I think that might have something to do with her trying to blame his death on me. At the time, I thought she really meant it. But now I realize that she said it out of anger and that she was afraid to face the reality that my father had a drinking problem. I remember asking myself, "Why didn't I know about his drinking problem? Why couldn't I have helped him?" Now I'm trying to accept and rid myself of the pain, and also the resentment towards my mother. I feel that Alateen can and will help with these feelings. Even though there will always be a scar on my heart, Alateen helps me to talk about how I feel and it relieves a lot of stress.

Jim
Pennsylvania, U.S.A

Alateen has helped me in many ways such as accepting alcoholism as a disease and learning to live with it and to accept and admit I am powerless over alcohol, the alcoholic and others. I know today I cannot change others and that I can only change myself! I am what counts, I am important. So are you. Alateen has also given me self-confidence. I have learned to be more dependent on myself and less dependent on others.

Melanie
California, U.S.A.

A big way Alateen has helped me gain self-confidence is by my getting involved in service work. Just between you and me, I didn't like the words "service work." It just plainly seemed like work (which I never really liked). Anyway, I soon found out it could be interesting and very exciting. It's merely trying to keep unity going. Sometimes it can make you feel good to give back a little in return. I feel I owe a lot to Alateen. So, I try and get involved. I am presently the treasurer for the Alateen conference for Southern Ontario and I am also the treasurer of my home group. Remember, the next time you hear anything about service work don't be frightened, go for it! Accept it!

Sandi
Ontario, Canada

I have been in Alateen for several years. My father has been sober for 11 years. I missed the worst of his drinking but my three older brothers and sisters didn't. Although I missed it, Alateen has still helped me to know that it wasn't my mother, brother or sister's fault that he drank. It helped me to accept it!

I go to an Alateen meeting with only four steady members but no matter if we have four or forty members, it still helps me. I hope Alateen has helped you!

Amy
Wisconsin, U.S.A.

I was full of hate and had no love for anyone. I used to make myself pretty so others would think something of me. The Serenity Prayer has helped me the most because I have to accept myself and others. Today I like other people and I have more friends. I've learned not to judge others and not to blame the alcoholic. Love is in my life now because I'm doing something about it.

Susanne
Mooroopna, South Australia

There are three members and one Sponsor in our group. We have been meeting for two years now. We started with a large group at the beginning, but as time went on we found only three of us wanted it bad enough to keep going.

We have learned we cannot change anyone but we have to accept them as they are. We can share our problems and help and listen to each other. Alateen is for all children of alcoholics and every child deserves to understand.

By going to other meetings, we shared what we have learned from the program, from each other and from ourselves. We put posters up around town and Conference Approved Literature in our school and left our names and numbers with the people in charge for anyone who needs us. We started having joint meetings with Al-Anon and have learned how to relate and learn from them for we found they need us and we need them. We have learned to accept the disease and that it can only be arrested but not cured.

We all care for Alateen so much, that's why we are writing and sharing ourselves with you.

Alateen Members
Saskatchewan, Canada

I've been in Alateen for one year. During the year, many good and bad things have happened to me. With Alateen, I have learned to appreciate the good things more and handle the bad things better.

I still get into trouble but it helps to know that I have a place to go. I can talk about my problems without people laughing at me or repeating what I said.

Alateen helps me cope with the disease of alcoholism. I don't like the disease, but there is nothing I can do about it. Now I know that the disease is both mental and physical. Nothing I say or do can make people stop drinking—only the will to stop and the courage to carry on can make someone stop.

Being a child or relative of an alcoholic is a misfortune, and I will always be a child of an alcoholic. I don't like it but I know that there is nothing I can do about it. Alateen helps.

Adrian
California, U.S.A.

I am very grateful to the program and to show this I gave service to the group. I'm not going to give a speech on service, yet I cannot stress enough that this area of my life is very special. When I began the program, I saw a light of hope, saying "Everything is going to be okay." My life has turned around tremendously in the last year and I thank my Higher Power I have a program and true friends. I have slipped many times since starting in the program six years ago and again I am slowly feeling the happiness that makes me glow.

My parents separated last year. Although I don't live with the alcoholic, I still go to Alateen because I know I was affected by the disease. Being out of the situation gave me a new perspective to my life. I realized that the coping with my dad was not the hard part. I had to see my mom was also affected by this disease. I'm learning to pray for her. I also pray to my Higher Power so my resentments will be released, and I try to "Let Go and Let God." I need this program.

So, for those Alateens who think Alateen is not for them, Keep Coming Back. One day it will hit you and you'll look back at yourself and say, "Is this really me?"

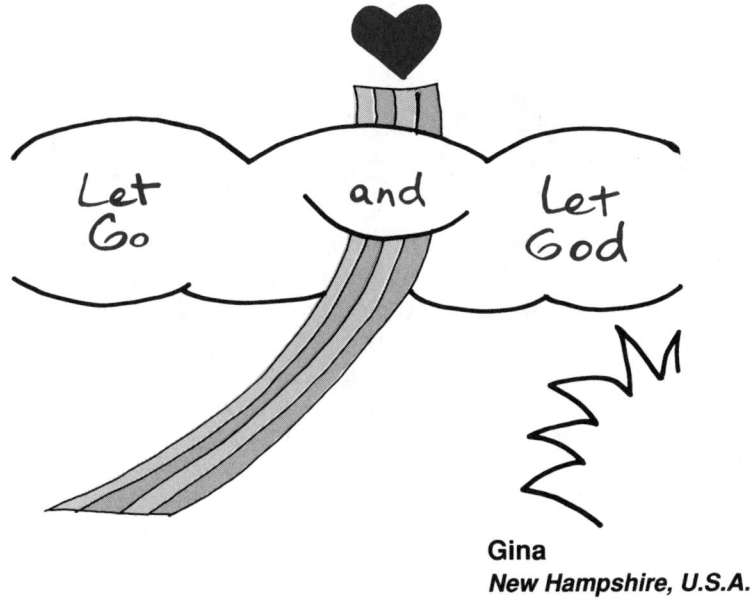

Gina
New Hampshire, U.S.A.

You'll look in the mirror and see a person with a smile and a look of inner peace, acceptance and happiness. Then extend this feeling to others and something wonderful happens. The feeling doubles! Take care Alateens and I love every one of you.

Caroline
Ontario, Canada

I am 12 years of age—I now live with my dad. My real mom and dad used to drink until they found a place to go for treatment. My brother and I stayed with my aunt and uncle for a while. My family and I went through a lot together; the good times and bad. Then I found Alateen through a friend and family member of the group. Before I was very afraid to tell people about my life and now through acceptance I know I don't have to be. I made a lot of friends in Alateen, and I thank all the people for helping me and my parents get to a place of recovery.

Deara
Kansas, U.S.A.

Alateen has made me a happier person, I am able to laugh at things that I would have gotten mad at before. Now I understand a lot more and make friends because I am happier. The main thing is that I have learned to accept the fact that I have an alcoholic in my family. I can do nothing about this person's drinking and I must make myself the best life possible. It all boils down to the Serenity Prayer and accepting the things I cannot change.

Jim
Missouri, U.S.A.

My first Alateen meeting was pretty scary. I went because my best friend asked me to, and I also needed some guidelines to live by. The people there were so nice and open—I found myself relating to many of their problems and concerns. I didn't know that I'd be welcomed as easy as I was and accepted for me. Ever since then, my life has changed and it keeps getting better.

Anne Marie
Ohio, U.S.A.

My Alateen sponsor encouraged me to share about Alateens who have become part of Al-Anon. I knew when she mentioned it that I had to write and share my own beautiful experience.

I started in Alateen when I was eight years old and it opened up a whole new world for me. I started to learn about alcoholism and to realize that my parents' drinking problem was not my fault. After I was in the program about six years I started getting involved in service work and became the group representative (GR) for my home group. In my seventh year I attended my first NO MAAC (Northern Mid-Atlantic Alateen Conference). I will never forget the feelings of love and acceptance I found there. About six months after the conference I felt as if I had learned all I could in Alateen and my sponsor suggested that I start attending Al-Anon. When I walked into the meeting I was so scared that I wouldn't be accepted as I was in Alateen. Boy, was I wrong. They treated me with such warmth and understanding that I felt my Higher Power had reopened all those closed doors, one more time! After a couple of Al-Anon meetings I was able to return to my Alateen meeting and grow in both Alateen and Al-Anon—what a reward.

Recently I celebrated my one year anniversary in Al-Anon and my eight year anniversary in Alateen. I thank God every day for giving me the tools of this program to make my life more manageable. Love and thanks,

Kelly
Pennsylvania, U.S.A.

Alateen is a program of growth. One of the first things we have to accept is that we cannot sober up our parents, and this is growth! Because we accept this, we open a door for ourselves.

If our parents were already sober when we entered Alateen, this was an added bonus; however, growth was still ahead of us. We learned to deal with our fears, resentments, angers and expectations the Alateen way, One Day at a Time.

Dear God, please help me to remember that my parents are people, too; to remember that the alcoholic is sick and so am I. Help me to live today.

Dani
California, U.S.A.

Be gentle with yourself...

and know that you are SPECIAL!

Pat
Nevada, U.S.A

Hi—I am the daughter of an alcoholic. Through Alateen I have learned to grow and cope with my problems. I love Alateen because I know the friends I have here love me and accept me for who I am.

Carolyn, Group Representative
Victoria, Australia

Before I came to Alateen my life was miserable. I could never tell my mom or dad how I felt about them. I could never tell Mom, "I don't like Dad to drink." Then I came to Alateen. At first I was scared, I thought everyone would make fun of me for what I said. But, instead they listened to me. I have been in the program for about a year and a half and my life has gotten better. My life is not totally perfect; I still have ups and downs, but I am able to express my feelings to other people like my mom, dad, sister and friends.

Josiah
Arizona, U.S.A.

I've just had one of the most exciting experiences of my life, I went to my first Alateen conference. I was scared at first, meeting so many new and different people. I didn't think they were going to like me because I considered myself a very unlikable person. It seemed as if it was going to be a long and depressing weekend. Then I noticed something, everyone was happy, smiling and giving hugs; everyone except me. It turned out the only person who didn't love and accept me was me! I am now engulfed in the glorious knowledge that I'm someone special.

Alateen conferences, have and will continue to influence my life.

Tony
Ohio, U.S.A.

Anonymous
Florida, U.S.A.

This picture is what brought me to meetings. When I would be upset or depressed about my dad, my mother would always know. I used to go to my room and cry or throw things. One day my mother came into my room and handed me this picture. She sat me down and explained that my father was sick, with a disease called alcoholism. My father always made promises that he never kept. Alateen helped me realize that it's not really my father talking. Instead it is a bottle that smells bad and makes you sick. I have learned to accept the things I cannot change and to have the courage to change the things I can. I am now grateful for all the things Alateen has to offer. I hope this picture will help someone understand the disease of alcoholism. I just want to say thank you.

Justine
Connecticut, U.S.A.

broken homes
broken bottles
broken promises
leads to
broken hearts

Before Alateen
I was grumpy
and mad . . . .

Thank you, Alateen
for helping me
feel happy and glad.

John
Florida, U.S.A.

When I first came to the program, I heard that I should be grateful for my parents, my group and the alcoholic. I understood that I should be thankful for my group and parents, but I did not understand why I was supposed to have gratitude for the alcoholic.

I've been in the Alateen program for six years and I've finally come to believe that I have gratitude for the alcoholic 'cause, without him, I wouldn't know of this way of life. This took four years of my group telling me until I was ready to accept it. Thanks for the patience, Alateen; I finally understand. Without you, I'd still have hateful feelings towards the alcoholic.

Bruce
Ohio, U.S.A.

My transition from Alateen to Al-Anon was smooth and comfortable. Although I had moments of awkwardness during the onset of my transition, I practiced the principles of my program which helped me to accept and to "Keep Coming Back."

I ventured into Al-Anon by encouragement and support from my Alateen group sponsor. My sponsor invited me to "speak" at Al-Anon meetings and soon I found myself being asked to chair at Al-Anon meetings. This was the beginning of my growth in Al-Anon and my growth as an adult.

In my Al-Anon growth I have surprised many with what knowledge and wisdom I have gained at such an early age. Many older Al-Anons have admitted their envy of my maturity and wisdom. But, what I need to keep in mind and stress to others is that it's not how old you are, but rather how well you practice the program. I need to keep in mind that my growth depends upon "keeping it simple, One Day at a Time, but letting it begin with me!"

Gregg
Pennsylvania, U.S.A.

Hi, I am a member of Alateen. I have been in the program now for over a year and plan to continue for more years to come.

My dad has been an alcoholic for as long as I can remember. Not long ago I finally realized that he may never change. Alateen has helped me to accept that and deal with it. Alateen has also helped me to deal with the anger, guilt, pain and disappointment of living with an alcoholic.

I find Alateen one of the most supporting groups I've been in. If I am having trouble with my alcoholic, Alateen is there for me and ready to support me. The support is strong and the love felt in the group makes me feel like a special and wanted person — something I never felt at home.

I spent a lot of times arguing with the alcoholic when I know now that arguing doesn't get you anywhere. I also spent a lot of time hoping he would change and trying to change him. I know now the only person I can change is me. I am still trying to change myself by not letting the

alcoholic affect my mood. At one time if he was drunk, I would get down; there were also a lot of broken promises and I'd feel disappointed. I have seen a big change in me since I've been with Alateen. Today, if a promise is broken, I try to think realistically. I am also trying not to be an enabler.

Alateen means a lot to me and I try not to miss a meeting. When things are going well and I don't have anything to talk about, I still go to support someone else who may need someone to talk to. I know at Alateen meetings people listen and understand because they can relate to my feelings of living with an alcoholic. They provide a lot of support and keep everything I say in confidence. I know that I can trust the group and feel free to say what's on my mind and in my heart. Alateen has helped me to deal with my feelings, with the alcoholic, and it's helped me to accept the things I cannot change.

Angela
Minnesota, U.S.A.

1. What does acceptance mean to you?

2. When you're feeling sorry for yourself, how does acceptance help you?

3. How do you accept criticism from someone else?

4. Does loving yourself come easier when you are accepted by other Alateen members?

5. How does acceptance relate to the First Step?

ALATEEN MEETING TOPICS

6. How do you accept yourself?

7. How do you relate acceptance to loving your family?

8. How do you accept group conscience when you don't agree with it?

9. How does Alateen literature help you to accept your situation?

10. How does accepting the disease of alcoholism make life easier?

Books and other pamphlets which may be of help:

BOOKS

- B-3 *Alateen—Hope for Children of Alcoholics*
- B-6 *One Day at a Time in Al-Anon* (Original size)
- B-8 *Al-Anon's Twelve Steps & Twelve Traditions*
- B-9 *Forum Favorites*, Vols. 1, 2, 3, and 4
- B-10 *Alateen—A Day at a Time*
- B-15 *. . . In All Our Affairs: Making Crises Work For You*
- B-23 *Courage To Be Me—Living With Alcoholism*

PAMPHLETS

- P-17 *Twelve Steps and Traditions*
- P-18 *Twelve Steps and Twelve Traditions for Alateen*
- P-59 *Moving On! From Alateen to Al-Anon*
- P-62 *Al-Anon Is For Adult Children of Alcoholics*
- P-64 *Alateen's 4th Step Inventory* (Workbook)
- P-69 *Serenity* (Booklet)
- P-70 *Slogans* (Booklet)

For Meeting Information:
1-888-4AL-ANON (USA)
On the Internet: http//www.al-anon.alateen.org

Al-Anon or Alateen may be listed in your telephone directory.